Dear Parent:
Your child's love of reading starts here!

Every child learns to read in a different way and at his or her own speed. Some go back and forth between reading levels and read favorite books again and again. Others read through each level in order. You can help your young reader improve and become more confident by encouraging his or her own interests and abilities. From books your child reads with you to the first books he or she reads alone, there are I Can Read Books for every stage of reading:

SHARED READING
Basic language, word repetition, and whimsical illustrations, ideal for sharing with your emergent reader

BEGINNING READING
Short sentences, familiar words, and simple concepts for children eager to read on their own

READING WITH HELP
Engaging stories, longer sentences, and language play for developing readers

READING ALONE
Complex plots, challenging vocabulary, and high-interest topics for the independent reader

ADVANCED READING
Short paragraphs, chapters, and exciting themes for the perfect bridge to chapter books

I Can Read Books have introduced children to the joy of reading since 1957. Featuring award-winning authors and illustrators and a fabulous cast of beloved characters, I Can Read Books set the standard for beginning readers.

A lifetime of discovery begins with the magical words "I Can Read!"

Visit www.icanread.com for information
on enriching your child's reading experience.

For Treeske. Enjoy!
—R.S.

I Can Read Book® is a trademark of HarperCollins Publishers.

ISBN 978-0-06-229425-8 (trade bdg.) — ISBN 978-0-06-229424-1 (pbk.)

15 16 17 18 19 SCP 10 9 8 7 6 5 4 3 2 1 ❖ First Edition

Splat the Cat

and the
Quick Chicks

Based on the bestselling books by Rob Scotton

Cover art by Rick Farley

Text by Laura Driscoll

Interior illustrations by Robert Eberz

HARPER

An Imprint of HarperCollinsPublishers

Splat's class had class pets.

Twelve chicken eggs!

Very soon they would hatch.

Then they would be chicks!

Mrs. Wimpydimple asked,
"Would someone take the eggs
home to watch tonight?"
Quick as a wink,
every paw flew up.

"We'll pick sticks,"

Mrs. Wimpydimple said.

"Whoever picks the longest stick

takes home the chicks."

One by one,

every cat picked a stick.

Plank picked a long stick.

Kitten picked a longer stick.

Splat picked

the longest stick of all!

Hooray!

Mrs. Wimpydimple helped Splat
get the eggs packed up.

"Just keep an eye on them
and keep them warm,"
said Mrs. Wimpydimple.
"That will do the trick!"

Splat carried the eggs home,

slowly and carefully.

No skips.

No kicks.

No quick, sudden moves along the way.

Splat made the chicks
a cozy nest in his drawer.
At bedtime, Splat said,
"Good night, chicks!"
and turned out the light.
Click!

Early the next morning,

Splat woke with a start.

He felt a peck on his ear.

He felt a tickle on his foot!

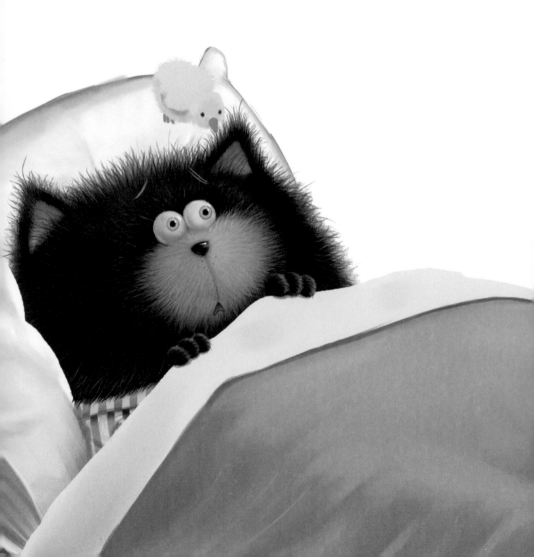

Splat looked in the nest.

The eggs had hatched!

The chicks were out and about.

Two chicks were on Splat.

But where were the rest?

Cheep! Cheep!

Splat's ears pricked up.

He followed the sound.

He found two chicks

in his thick, warm socks.

16

Splat found two more chicks
snuggled up to the clock.
Tick-tick-tick . . .

Splat looked in his toy corner.

There was a chick in a truck.

There was a chick

in Splat's magic-trick box.

One chick was sitting
in the paint box.

Ick.

And there were two chicks in the house
made of snap-together bricks.

Splat had found eleven chicks.

But one was still missing.

Splat was worried sick.

Then Splat heard a

pick-peck-pick.

He turned around

in the nick of time.

There was the last chick!

It picked and pecked at the basket.

Then it hopped away.

The other chicks went with it.

"Stop, chicks!" said Splat.

Splat chased chicks up . . .

and chased chicks down.

Chicks fell in.

But chicks hopped out.

Wet feathers drip, drip, dripped.

Splat stepped into a puddle.

SPLAT!

The chicks stood all
over Splat.
"We better get to school
before you run away again!"
said Splat.

Splat led the way.

The chicks followed

each move.

With skips
and kicks,
the good little chicks
got to school lickety-split!

Splat's class was so surprised!
Instead of twelve eggs,
now there were—

"Eleven chicks?" said Mrs. Wimpydimple.

"Splat, where is the missing chick?"

Oh no! thought Splat.

But before he could get worried sick,

Splat heard a cheep.

"Phew!" said Splat.

"These chicks *are* quick!"